Earth Ways:
Healing Medicine for the Soul

A PRACTICAL GUIDE FOR CEREMONIES FOR THE EARTH

Sonja Grace

Contents

$\mathcal{E}$arth Ways Mission Statement

As a warrior of the light, your greatest path is to surrender to your own resistance.

Do not succumb to your fear, for it is fear itself that manifests before your eyes . . .

Carry the sword of light and make claim to nothing in this world, as we are but visitors creating higher energy in physical form.

Honor the Goddess for it is her life, the Earth that sustains us and keeps us alive.

Heal all of the imperfections you see in others within yourself, and hold true to the knowledge that if you heal yourself, you will heal the world.

Introduction

Throughout history, humans have celebrated life and the seasons with ritual and ceremony. These sacred words and songs have marked time and uncovered a depth of spiritual wealth for people everywhere.

In the 21st century, however, we have become disconnected from our feelings. The pure essence of daily ritual is lost. Many of us feel a sense of longing and a need to connect with the elements once again. Giving back to the Earth acknowledges that she is alive and is a living being, as are all things on the Earth. To see her in any other state is to deny the very core of our own existence.

Earth Ways provides a series of prayers, meditations and insights about the Earth's seasons that can be practiced on a daily basis, offering a connection to the source. As with all ceremonies, it is important that your intention is clear, for that is truly what makes any ceremony powerful. You must ensure that your will is in alignment with the Goddess and the Universe before performing any of these prayers and ceremonies.

I stood in the dark with the hood of my coat pulled up over my head, wrapped in a wool blanket that encased me like a cocoon. The stars were out and a long line of women waited while the men prepared. My eyes watered as I smelled burning wood mixed with coal. I looked up and felt as if I was in the center of the universe. No one talked; there was just the sound of the wind gently blowing across the landscape. It was an honor to be there and to stand with these women. It was unheard of and I felt the Earth creep into my skin and ground me as if I had been standing there for centuries. There was a light and we moved inside.

$\mathcal{F}$rom the Past to the Present

There is a primal reason so many people around the world gravitate to Native American culture. We hear their music and feel moved at such a deep level it is as if a memory is triggered from our very own past. We see their art and feel deep connections to the Earth we cannot explain. We hear their language and something inside of us remembers a time we walked with them. We smell the cedar burning and our very souls feel cleansed.

Native Americans are not 'Dancing with Wolves.' Native Americans are fighting for their very lives and what little land they have. Gangs, drugs, alcohol and abuse occur every day on reservations around the United States. Their land, sacred to them, is being robbed of natural resources and once again we face pollution and destruction of our sacred Mother Earth.

It is important to keep alive the beauty and rich cultures of all Native Americans. The ceremonies that have kept families and villages thriving for centuries provide an understanding of ways taught only within those cultures. Native people often regard their ceremonies as private, just like any other religion. Many tribes have rites of passage for young people and initiations into various religious societies. In most cases these initiates are not allowed to share with others. Different clans hold different parts to these ceremonies and asking questions is often inappropriate. The rituals are private, like certain ceremonies held by a priest or rabbi.

So what does an entire culture of Caucasian-European mixed-blooded people do about their feelings for Native culture? They learn respect first and foremost. They ask permission before walking into a plaza, kiva, sweat lodge or ceremony. They find the visitors center and read the rules, and if there are any questions they ask an adult. People often do not understand that children do not know some of the answers because they have not yet been initiated into that knowledge. The most important part of this understanding is to realize everyone has connections to Earth Ways that are from past lives that go beyond Native America.

Around the world in any culture it is best to understand that you do not practice another culture's ceremonies without permission. You do not burn cedar without understanding the spirit of the Cedar and why it is used. You do not beat the drum and sing Native songs without permission and the utmost reverence for the gift that was given to you. Picking up a drum and creating your own song from the heartbeat of the Earth is a whole different story. But taking another's culture and calling it your own is crossing lines that can bring pain and suffering to a people that have already endured enough.

We all come from these Earth Ways, and the path of the white man is the most difficult as remembering these deep roots inside of us is something many fight and others reject and want to sell. White culture carries a pain inside from having these Earth Ways taken from them long ago. Many Native Americans feel this, too, as they have past lives in European culture. People feel a separation from the Earth, which is a collective consciousness from lifetimes of being denied the Goddess. Many people have died for these Earth Ways, and continue to carry the karma into this life in effort to heal.

A soulfulness inherent in Indigenous cultures allows everyone to take life a bit slower . . . not rush past the moment. There is a deeper connection to the land, the sea, the mountains and sky that our past lives echo through many time periods where we fought, starved and prayed for the sake of our people and our land.

Most Native Americans just smile and never let you know you have gone into a sacred area, crossed a border where no one goes, walked into a ceremony uninvited. They will say nothing and take their grievance back to their village. There, they might cry to a relative that the white man just continues to take and does not respect their ways. Another person may get angry and wish to have what the white man in town has, and yet another might drink and drug to numb their pain to a point that they don't return home and are found dead in the wild.

This is not a case where white culture needs to once again feel responsible for something that happened long before many of us were born. The enabling of many reservations comes from the government putting tribes in the middle of nowhere with no supporting industries close at hand. Many tribes have already integrated the current trends of society and created success for their people. These tribes are sharing their culture through tours and experiences visitors can have without compromising their ceremonies and deep cultural ways.

In all of the spiritual evolution ever-present in our world, we continue to look to Native Americans for inspiration and a belief that we are still connected. We all want to believe that Kevin Costner became a part of the Sioux tribe he so fell in love with in 'Dances with Wolves.' Integrated marriage of other races and cultures within Native America blends our worlds together like a fine weaving.

It is up to the European immigrants in this country to honor these people and respect their ways. That means when you hear the drum and feel the rhythm of the Earth moving through your feet, up your legs and into your heart, you will move from the place in you that is humble, respectful and willing to wait until you are in a place that is right for you to do so.

American culture is all about getting something now. We have not learned from a place of having had to wait for anything. Native Americans have all grown up waiting; they wait to go home because they were sent off to boarding school and not allowed to speak their language. They wait to get a job and it never comes. They wait to have a home and it is never built. They wait for the snow to melt so they can get down the road. They are always waiting and demonstrating a kind of patience that white culture is as far from as we are from the moon.

The global New Age culture has produced many people who feel connected to spirit and the Earth. There is awareness that there is much more to the Universe than what we were told as children, and a deep feeling among many that we are highly sensitive beings. It is only natural that this group gravitates toward the truth and what is connected to the heart of all living things: the Earth.

Introducing the red road to this culture of people has been popular, but often misunderstood. There can be an interpretation of Native American culture that is displayed without thought of permission or respect for those who still to this day carry these ways and are in fact the keepers of these sacred things. Non-native people have come into Native villages and written books and taken pictures and never asked permission to do so. Some have asked permission, but even so, there is always someone who is not happy.

Can we make everyone happy? Not usually, in any culture around the world. But we can recognize what is someone else's business and what is our own. We can create a connection to the Mother Earth through our own prayers and respect for her without taking someone else's ways. We can appreciate the Indian culture and share in that culture if we are invited to do so. The key word is "invited." There are people everywhere who feel a sense of entitlement and righteous ownership of all land and material things. This is not the way of Native Americans, and their land is sacred to them. There are places on their land no one should walk, for they believe there are other things there that are so sacred no one even talks about it. The spirit realm is real to many indigenous people and the knowledge that spirits exist and are walking with us during certain times of the year is common sense in their understanding.

The New Age culture has gravitated towards several modalities of thinking, the most popular being Shamanism. The power a person can feel from moving about the realms is enticing and it is a way to bring all of the sensitivity back into order so that it makes sense. In some cases, it is a direct way to heal a past life during which a person might have suffered from a difficult outcome due to the practices of Shamanism.

In American culture, people sometimes seek out shamanistic ways that without proper training can lead to a state of assumptions. Many difficult passages to gaining awareness and abilities are skipped to reach that power point. It's best to find proper training with a teacher who understands and respects the boundaries of another culture.

In Native culture there are rites of passage and ways that people earn the honor to carry a pipe or take part in a ceremony. There are steps that teach us humility first, and then another level of humility, and once you have learned a little more, you learn more humility. In the Lakota tradition, when a person goes on Hanjblecceya or vision quest they fast without food and water for four days while praying with a sacred pipe and asking Great Spirit for a vision. It is not an easy thing to do and they learn quickly what is most important in life: Water.

This act of humility through prayer is a great example of what can be missed when a person runs to learn how to be a shaman and potentially misses the true lessons.

As I sat on the floor I could feel the heat from the wood stove pressing in on me. We were all close together as a group and community. The room was pitch black and you could hear a sound that came out of nowhere all on its own. The sound came to each of us as if we were being touched by the energy itself.

What seemed like forever was only a short time and when I arrived I had a new name.

The floor was damp and the smell of smoke filled my lungs. I crawled in the dark waiting for the heat to rise and fill my bones. This was something I remembered from long ago. I saw the old ones come in and smile at me when I made my prayers. They told me not to worry; all of our prayers were heard and she was listening. They said to love her and protect her from all of the harm that she endures daily. They said this planet was sacred. In the scheme of the Universe, it was considered one of the sacred gems. The ancient voices continued with the reminder of why we come here to Earth in human form. They said it is to resolve our inner conflicts and gain understanding that we are in our true form in spirit and the body is just a tool. I sang my song loud and with a strength that came from deep inside my soul.

Spring

In Earth Ways we acknowledge that the Creator, the Universe, the Goddess and the Earth receive your prayers. The energy from above and the energy from below meet halfway and join within you, for you are the physical conduit that receives this divine energy. The Earth protects us and provides the elements we need to survive. She is an immense being and is the very essence of what we are made of: Water.

Earth is known as the "Blue Planet" because 71 percent of the Earth's surface is covered with water. Even with so much water surrounding us, we need to remember that water is a finite resource. Water is part of Earth's closed system; very little matter leaves or enters the atmosphere. In practical terms, this means that the water you drink today might be the same water that once trickled down the back of a wooly mammoth, floated Cleopatra's royal barge down the Nile or formed part of the iceberg that sank the Titanic.

The hydrologic cycle cleans and replenishes the water supply. The Earth has an abundance of water, but less than one percent is usable by humans for drinking water. The other 99 percent is in the oceans, soils, icecaps, and floating in the atmosphere.

Visible bodies of water are referred to as surface water. The majority of fresh water is actually found underground as soil moisture and in aquifers. Groundwater feeds streams, which is why a river can keep flowing even when there has been no precipitation, and is also why most water used by humans comes from rivers.

Earth Ways: Prayer for Water

Bring a container of water outside with you. Pour some into your hand and hold it carefully, for it is precious. Say your prayer in silence as if the water is absorbing your words. Thank the Earth for all of the water on the planet. Ask that it continue to flow clean with an abundance of life. Now, give your prayer to the Earth. Let the water that holds your prayer seep down into the Earth and release it. Experience this prayer next to a tree or plant and give your offering to it.

In the spring we gather our seeds and prepare to plant, bringing new life and a new cycle to our lives and the place we live on the Earth. This planting cycle is a renewal, and it is the true beginning of the New Year. We have many seasonal experiences in which change creates the new order for the following three month period. Spring is often linked to words such as fever and madness; music celebrates rites of spring and is used in fertility ceremonies.

The Earth reflects to us daily that she is in pain. As a result we witness her shifting and reshaping her surface to turn the soil as we would in a garden. She is missing so many key components that help her stay healthy and vibrant. We can participate in this restructuring by using our energy to help rebuild the Earth.

Earth Ways: Ceremony for the Earth

Stand outside and quietly thank the Earth for all she provided during the past year. Feel your energy grounding into her right through the soles of your feet. Say your prayers into your hand, as if you are holding the words cupped in your palm. Place your hand on the Earth, and release your prayers with a hand motion that sweeps across the Earth. This is where heaven and Earth meet and your prayers are sprinkled in between.

Earth Ways: A Prayer to the Earth

Thank you, Mother Earth, for the air I breathe, the ground I walk on, the silence in the night, the cold wind on my face and the bright colors of spring. I recognize these are your gifts and I am grateful. My heart is filled with love as I send rays of love to my inner core; I also send rays of love deep down into the ground, filling you, Mother Earth, with my gratitude. May I create peace upon your land and care for you the way I care for my children and loved ones. May I walk softly so that I might hear your song and celebrate in your beauty each and every day.

Spring Equinox

The Spring Equinox is one of the four great solar festivals of the year. Day and night are equal, poised and balanced, but about to tip over on the side of light. The Spring Equinox is sacred to dawn, youth, the morning star and the east. The Saxon goddess, Eostre (from whose name we get the direction East and the holiday Easter) is a dawn goddess, like Aurora and Eos. Just as the dawn is the time of new light, so the vernal equinox is the time of new life.

The New Year

In many traditions, this is the start of the new year. The Roman year began on the ides of March (15th). The astrological year begins on the equinox when the moon moves into the first sign of the Zodiac, Aries, the Ram. The Greek god Ares was the forerunner of the Roman god Mars, for whom the month of March is named. Between the 12th century and 1752, March 25th was the day the year changed in England and Ireland. March 25, 1212 was the day after March 24, 1211.

The Arrival of Spring

Although we saw the first promise of spring at Candlemas (February second) in the swelling buds, there were still nights of frost and darkness ahead. Now spring is manifest. Demeter is reunited with her daughter, Persephone (the essence of spring), who has been in the Underworld for six months and the earth once again teems with life. The month of March contains holidays dedicated to all the great mother goddesses: Astarte, Isis, Aphrodite, Cybele and the Virgin Mary. The goddess shows herself in the blossoms, the leaves on the trees, the sprouting of the crops, the mating of birds, the birth of young animals. In the agricultural cycle, it is time for planting. We are assured that life will continue.

As always in birth, there can be fear in the passage that brings in life. For those moments of fear, we can look to an easy prayer of passage.

Earth Ways: Prayer for Fear

Help me, Mother Earth, to release my fears down through my body, down my legs, out my feet and into the ground. Down my arms, out my hands and into the ground. Let your energy come back up through my body, grounding my body and nurturing my soul. Let my love fill the spaces where I doubted the universe. Thank you for your endless beauty.

Earth Ways: Prayer for the Spring

In the Spring we plant our seeds into your rich soil, Mother Earth. Thank you for your love and nurturing as they grow into the very food that will feed us and the grain that feeds all of us around the world. We are humbled by you, Goddess, as you provide our essential needs for life. As I send this prayer deep into your ground, I ask that this New Year be filled with harmony, love, good health and prosperity for everyone around the world. I ask that you receive my seeds with these prayers for my Earth family.

Earth Ways: Ceremony for Clearing your Energy with the Earth

Bring the Earth's energy up through the bottom of your feet and feel it swirl and cleanse your root chakra. Next, feel that energy rise and swirl through your second chakra or belly center. Now, feel it travel up through the third chakra into your solar plexus cleansing your power center. Feel the Earth's energy move into your heart and cleanse and purify your center for love. Now feel your throat and the fifth chakra being cleansed and allow that energy to swirl into the sixth chakra

clearing your mind. Feel it travel all the way to the top of your head and clear the seventh chakra. Feel the Earth's energy move back down through your body taking all that it has cleared into the Earth herself and release it out of the bottom of your feet. Place your hands on the Earth and thank her for helping you to clear your energy centers!

Earth Ways: Ceremony for a Tree

Sit with your back to a tree and feel your roots going deep into the ground, just as the tree's do. Ask the tree spirit to help you remove any tension in your body, dissolving it into the Earth. Ask the tree spirit to connect you above to the Universe and to help you gain the consciousness of the tree connecting above and below, experiencing the union of heaven and Earth. Feel the energy of the tree and be still with the understanding that you are receiving spiritually from above and below. When you are done, place your hand on the tree and give your gratitude for all of the help you have received.

Earth Ways: Prayer for the Birds

Thank you, Mother Earth, for providing such a beautiful home for the winged ones. Your safe harbor allows these birds to carry messages from their world into our world. They heal those who follow their flight and carry the fierce warrior within protecting our skies above. Thank you, Goddess, for the winged ones.

Earth Ways: Prayer for the House Plant

With this tiny bit of soil, I am humble before you, Mother Earth, and ask for your blessing on this day. I am forever grateful for your beauty and shelter and ask that you help me to be guided in the direction I need to go. I ask that you help me to manifest what is for my highest good here on your land and with this small bit of soil; I ask that you give me a sign today. My heart is like a three dimensional sun with rays of love shining out to you, Mother Earth, and rays of love shining into myself.

Earth Ways: Prayer for Mothers

It is with the deepest gratitude that we thank you, Goddess, for all of the Mothers who have brought life to this Earth. We observe you each and every day creating life that overwhelms the senses and brings us to the heart of miracles.

The Earth is our most humble reminder of how fragile we are. We reincarnate to experience our passage of love through spiritual evolution and consciousness. We pray to have your strength and resilience and to offer the same respect to our Mothers that we offer to you.

When we are born, our lives are dependent upon these sacred women who sacrifice their bodies, minds and spirits so that we will live until we are able to survive on our own. We recognize that you make this sacrifice daily.

The Earth is always our Mother, and it is with all of the love in our hearts that we thank you and our own Mother for our lives.

The Four Seasons and the Chakras

Each season is associated with one or more chakra energies. Here's a brief overview.

The first chakra is reflected in the winter. The survival issues of food, clothing and shelter help us move into the Spring and the second chakra of procreation and planting seeds within the womb. The Summer leads us into the third chakra and feeling the power of ourselves and the sun along with the close ties we have to the Universe. In the fall we have a golden energy that comes through the auric field and we are more open in the fourth chakra of the body. This doesn't mean we love more in the fall, as we experience spring fever and winter warmth along with summer love! Rather, on an energy level, we experience more connection to that chakra during that season. The fifth chakra relates to the Earth, and as we move into the fifth dimension, we will experience speaking up where we have not in the past and feel more connected with other realms and hearing the subtler messages. The sixth chakra relates to the Sun and the energy the sun shines out to our solar system, warming the Earth as your third eye gazes upon all that you see. This center is the psychic realm and the sun sends us messages all the time, giving us that radiant opportunity to perceive what is at the core of our solar system. The seventh chakra relates to the moon and has a strong connection to that opening we feel to the divine. The moon reflects our feelings and at the same time represents an emotional connection to the Universe. This is the gateway to the upper chakras as the moon is the gateway to beyond the Earth.

Carry your feelings with the intent of processing, and be mindful as to what time of year it is and what is highlighted in the energy realms. Your energy is fine-tuned to each season and your body follows suit.

There was a strange smell from the trees early in the morning as the first birds sang their song with total conviction. The smell was a dampness warming in the sun and it reminded me of bread baking in my Grandmother's kitchen. I was cold and wrapped in a blanket, trying to get past my thoughts of hunger. There was a question of whether I was more hungry than thirsty, but it did not matter for I was avoiding my prayer. I went back to the sun and began again, hoping this time to ignore what my body realized gives me my life.

I sat quietly at the table with a respected sun dancer. She is a healer and her medicine is strong. She has helped many people on the red road, more than I think there are fences guarding this land. She does this with humility and respect for these Native ways. People came by, and like a swarm of mosquitoes they made a lot of noise and left, missing the opportunity. She has danced in the hot sun praying to the Creator for strength for her family and for her people. She has endured four days without food and water, merging with the spirit realm in order to help her people. She has suffered and given all she has to give so that her people can be strong.

I felt the breeze cross across my back and realized she was gone.

Summer

The summer represents a deep relaxation as humanity and all of Earth's creation bathe in the warmth of the sun as it melts away the cold of spring and winter. Ceremonies are in full swing during this time. We mark summer with vacations, sending our children to camp and time in and around water.

But the Earth marks summer as a time of fruition and the marriage between herself and the sun cultivating abundance for all who dwell upon her. She is at her full reign in the summer months and historically speaking the solstice carries a great passage for the season.

The summer solstice occurs exactly when the Earth's axial tilt is most inclined towards the sun at its maximum of 23° 26′. Though the summer solstice is an instant in time, the term is also colloquially used, such as Midsummer to refer to the day on which it occurs. Except in the Polar Regions (where daylight is continuous for many months during the spring and summer), the day on which the summer solstice occurs is the day of the year with the longest period of daylight. Thus the seasonal significance of the Summer solstice is in the reversal of the gradual shortening of nights and lengthening of days. The summer solstice occurs in June in the Northern Hemisphere and in December in the Southern Hemisphere. The word solstice comes from Latin sol (sun) and sistere (to stand still).

North of the Tropic of Cancer (23°26′N) and south of the Tropic of Capricorn (23°26′S), the Sun reaches its highest position in the sky on the day of the summer solstice. However, between the Tropic of Cancer and the Tropic of Capricorn, the highest sun position does not occur at the summer solstice, because the sun reaches the zenith here and it does so at different times of the year depending on the latitude of the observer. Depending on the shift of the calendar, the summer solstice occurs sometime between December 21 and December 22 each year in the Southern Hemisphere, and between June 20 and June 21 in the Northern Hemisphere.

Historical interpretation of the solstice has varied from culture to culture. Most cultures have held ceremonial recognitions of summer as a sign of Earth's fertility, including holidays, festivals, gatherings, rituals and other celebrations.

It has recently become a popular belief in the United States that the meteorological season of summer begins with the astronomical phenomenon of the summer solstice. Other regions reckon the start of summer to the beginning of the month of the solstice, or even the month preceding it.

Awed by the great power of the sun, civilizations have for centuries celebrated the first day of summer (variously called the Summer Solstice, Midsummer, St. John's Day or the Wiccan Litha).

The Celts and Slavs celebrated the first day of summer with dancing and bonfires to help increase the sun's energy. The Chinese marked the day by honoring Li, the Chinese Goddess of Light.

Perhaps the most enduring modern ties with Summer Solstice are the Druids' celebration of the day as the "wedding of Heaven and Earth," resulting in the present day belief of a "lucky" wedding in June.

Today, Midsummer is still celebrated around the world--most notably in England at Stonehenge and Avebury, where thousands gather to welcome the sunrise on the Summer Solstice. Pagan spirit gatherings or festivals are also common in June, when groups assemble to light a sacred fire, then stay up all night to welcome the dawn.

Pagans called the Midsummer moon the "Honey Moon" for the mead made from fermented honey that was part of wedding ceremonies performed at the Summer Solstice. They also celebrated Midsummer with bonfires. Couples would leap through the flames, believing their crops would grow as high as they were able to jump.

Midsummer was thought to be a time of magic, when evil spirits appeared. To thwart them, Pagans often wore protective garlands of herbs and flowers. One of the most powerful was a plant called 'chase-devil', which is known today as St. John's Wort and still used by modern herbalists as a mood stabilizer.

Earth Ways: Ceremony for the Summer Solstice

As you meet the dawn with your hand cupped with an offering of grain, pray to the Sun and give your thanks for the marriage of the Sun and the Earth. Offer this grain to the Earth and place it in the East as the Sun comes up. Place your hand on the Earth and give her your prayers for the health and happiness of your family and world community. Let rays of love fill up the Earth and all of her land. Feel the rays of the sun streaming through you and into the Earth and feel the Earth sending energy up through you and out to the Sun. Ask that your prayers be in alignment with this sacred marriage between the Sun and the Earth on this day.

Earth Ways: Prayer for the Summer

Goddess, we pray to you that the summer is filled with the abundance of what we planted in spring growing healthy and strong. We also pray for your winds to be calm and the water to be clean. May your life force fill all of our energy centers and may we give you the love and care you need. Let the summer months be filled with joy and abundance for your sacred land. Let the warmth of each day fill our hearts and minds reminding us of how sacred your land is and how grateful we are to be here.

Earth Ways: Prayer for the Water

Thank you, Mother Earth, for your rivers and oceans and for the abundance of life in your sacred waters. I am sending my gratitude like rays of sunshine from my heart into your oceans, rivers, and streams and filling every molecule with love. I pray for good health and help for your water, Mother Earth, for without you we would not be here. I am humbled by your presence and the beauty of this land. I am forever grateful for the water that quenches my thirst each and every day.

Earth Ways: Prayer for the Four-Legged Ones

Thank you, Goddess, for all that you provide for the four-legged ones that walk this sacred Earth. We are grateful for their lives and all the joy they bring us in friendship, family and guidance. These animals are the healing force we recognize and honor that nurture us daily. Without you,

Mother Earth, we would not survive. With this Earth Ways prayer we thank you for our furry relatives and the ones who walk with four legs.

Earth Ways: Prayer for a Blue Moon

In the light of this sacred moon I am giving thanks to the Earth for her love and kindness. I send my love and kindness back to her with the gratitude for all that she provides. With the moon illuminating all that is needed around the world, let those who have not be blessed with abundance and let the Earth herself be healed with rays of love from my heart deep into her body. Let all of my prayers for good health, happiness, prosperity and divine love be heard throughout the Universe and on this sacred Blue Moon.

Earth Ways: Ceremony for the Sun

At sunrise place a crystal, preferably clear quartz, in the path of the rising sun. Ask the Sun to fill up the crystal with Sun energy and light. Reach your hand out to the Sun and place it on your heart as you thank the Sun for all of the warmth and energy provided to the Earth. Once a full day has passed from sunrise to sunset bring the crystal into your home. Place the crystal in an area of your house that you feel is dark and needs light. Leave it there and renew this ceremony in the fall, winter and spring.

Water in the summer months is most precious and should be always respected and honored. The Earth's water has been recycled over millions of years and has touched the heavens as well as circulated around the world. It is from the deepest respect this prayer is done.

Earth Ways: Ceremony for Water

Take a cup of water outside and pray over that offering. Tell the Earth you want her to have a drink of water as she is always providing for you. After your prayers have gone into this water give this to the Earth and ask her to receive what has always been hers, but back to her again, with your prayers of good health and happiness for the Goddess.

The quiet sound of their singing voices carried over the landscape. Not quite barren, the Earth held little warmth with crisp air in and around the ancient rocks. We watched as the people approached with anticipation. Suddenly there were gifts flying through the air and all who needed received. I was thinking about the past and how many times we repeat what is meaningful and sacred.

Autumn

In the fall, the air grows crisp and we walk through leaves that stir memories of the past and thoughts of what is to come. We see the cycle of the year come to a close as the garden and all that flourished through Spring and Summer now returns to the Earth. It is a subtle death and reminds us of the seasons and how there is forever change here on Earth.

During this season, the Earth comes to a close with the completion of the main cycle of life. We feel our energy starting to wind down and prepare for the winter. As we shift so do our outer layers. The auric field is as much involved in the cycles of the Earth as are the tides of the ocean, sun and moon. The auric field goes through changes each season that are in relationship to these tides.

The fall becomes a transition from the celebration of the Earth's abundance to the harvest that is gathered in preparation for the coming months. We often start new projects as our children return back to school and another form of balance is restored. Spiritually, we are in preparation for the closure and death of many Earth bound flora and fauna. We are releasing the connection to what has just taken place above ground and preparing for everything to move underground. This transition can feel smooth with sharp edges as we create a pathway for the winter months ahead. During the fall we need to focus on our ability to release the past. Our understanding of death is a wonderful opportunity the Earth provides us each year. The best way for us to deal with our own death is to experience the mini deaths we are witnessing each autumn. This built in system the Earth provides allows us helps us to deal with everything that is changing in life. Ceremonies around the world celebrate the harvest and Autumn Equinox as it is a form of celebrating the death passage, through what might be experienced as mini deaths. The focus towards our spiritual connection with the

Earth leads us to a much richer understanding of the soul's journey. Through ceremonies and prayer we can redefine our passage by observing the Earth during her fall cycle. Humanity has reincarnated for lifetimes providing a karmic experience that is the crux of our spiritual evolution. The fall becomes an important marker for our spiritual growth connecting us to the ultimate passage: death. The Earth shows us death is a part of life and through her yearly seasons reminds us to not be attached to this physical form. It is our attachment that keeps us bound by our karmic experience and prevents us from our own evolution. Releasing our karma is what the trees do in the fall. We witness the trees gracefully releasing their leaves as they journey inward to reflect. We can let go of the karmic attachments like autumn leaves through forgiveness. By forgiving each other we stop incurring more karma and shift the spiritual process to our soul's enlightenment. Autumn also teaches us to let go of the past and trust in the process that winter will restore and spring renew. Despite the changes that the Earth makes it is with consistency she ebbs and flows as the tides of the ocean, sun and moon. She shows us by reflecting these tides in our own auric fields. The subtle energies of our spiritual body are experienced through the connection we make with the planet. She teaches us everything we need to know about accepting change in our lives. Our homework is to feel our feelings and provide continual care for Mother Earth. The mission statement for humanity is to love at the deepest level of our beings. With the fall providing this time to release we open to the opportunity to receive new energy.

Earth Ways: Prayer for the Autumn

In this conclusion of your vibrant summer I ask you, Mother Earth, to receive my gratitude for the harvest and all of the abundance that you provide. I ask that the ending of this cycle be blessed with the closure of your wisdom in helping us prepare for the winter. Your cool breeze and night time chill reminds me this is one door closing and the preparation for the next season. In this Autumn, I pray you help me to transition from the warm summer months to the cold winter days with the sun shortening my days. In gratitude I thank you, Goddess, for your support and send my love deep into your land.

Earth Ways: Prayer for a Full Moon

On this night we are grateful, Mother Earth, for your full moon illuminating the darkness and showing us all that needs to be seen. Our emotional bodies are one with the reflection of light that comes to us on this sacred eve and is a constant reminder of the light that lives within each one of us. We ask you, Mother Earth, to continue to bless us with the abundance of your food, shelter and warmth and we ask that you always remember how much we appreciate what you give us. It is with the deepest gratitude in our hearts that we thank you for your beauty, your light and your love. May the light of each one of us shine deeply into your sacred land.

Earth Ways: Prayer for the Shower

As you stand in the shower feeling the warm water cover your skin thank the Goddess for the abundance of water on Earth. Feel the water carrying all pain and illness from your body inside and out and feel it leaving your hands and the soles of your feet. Ask that your day begin anew with your heart and mind cleared by this sacred water. Ask that your day be filled with complete harmony and feel your whole body fill up with an abundance of peace and love.

Earth Ways: Ceremony for Your Home

Sit in meditation and feel the Earth beneath you, even if it is through the floor. Send your energy into the Earth and ground yourself. Feel Earth energy coming up into your body and supporting you in this process. Ask that the highest angels come and be with you in accordance with the will of God and the Goddess, for the highest good of everyone and the highest good of the Universe. Ask that your home be cleansed through the Earth's energy. Then ask that your home be filled with the highest vibration from the Universe and

that the white light descend and fill every inch of your home. Feel that energy surrounding your home with protection and love. Thank the angels for helping you with this blessing and thank the Goddess for lending her energy to support your home and all that is in it.

Earth Ways: Prayer for the Harvest

It is with the deepest gratitude that I thank you, Mother Earth, for my life and the continued abundance you provide. The air that I breathe and the water that I drink are all because of you and your wondrous abilities to create an environment I can live in. With this prayer I send my energy of love and healing to you, the Goddess, for we are all living on your land, near and far, asking that you receive this with the intention to give back to you. My corn is sweet, my squash is ripe and my tomatoes are in abundance...Thank you for this fall harvest and the opportunity to prepare for winter. Thank you for nourishing my family, my village and the world.

Earth Ways: Ceremony for the Cycle of Life

Sit on the Earth with leaves in both hands. Offer these leaves to the Goddess asking her to give you the ability to regenerate as the leaves do. Their cycle of birth in Spring and full glory in the Summer followed by death and decomposing back into the Earth in the Fall is the same as the human cycle of life. Ask that your body, mind and spirit understand that you, too, will someday be as the leaves and you want to embrace this knowledge so you can be more attuned to your own natural rhythm honoring the process of your life cycle.

Earth Ways: Ceremony for the Autumn Equinox

In meditation ask the Goddess for the Violet Flame to clear all of the negative energy in your body, auric field and home. Ask for clearing on all levels. Once you feel the energy lift from your body, continue by asking for the White Light to descend into your body, auric field and home. Ask next for the Golden Light and feel it fill every cell in your body, auric field and home. Then ask for the Blue Light to fill your mind, body and spirit and keep you. safe and protected.

Reaching across the table I could see her looking into my eyes. She was bright and beautiful. Her hair was long and framed her face like smoke rising up from the cedar. She was as big as the room and took up all of the space. My legs were shaking as I heard her voice speaking to me. I have come to thank you for your prayer. It is my intention to help you and give you the understanding of my body, the Earth. The Goddess was radiant in the room and I noticed all sound had stopped. All I could hear was her smooth and warm voice filling up all of the spaces inside my heart. She said she wanted to stay but was in a lot of pain with all that was happening on her surface and underground. She said in the old days, people around the world talked to her as they talked to

their own mothers, sharing their pain, love, joy and sadness. She said the Earth was her body much in the same way that we have bodies. After sometime of being in her presence, I got up from the table and went outside and cried as I held my hands to the ground with the realization she never asked me for anything.

The cold air reached inside of my head as we walked in the snow just before dawn. It was so quiet you could hear a pin drop. We walked the pathway to give our prayers to the sun. It was a feeling that was so ancient my bones ached. Tiny rays of light danced over the horizon and warmed my forehead. There were mostly women passing on the trail; the men were down below. The spirit realm was all around us, but no one spoke. It was personal and all about family.

inter

In the winter months, we walk quietly upon Mother Earth and recognize that this is a time when trees and plants have gone dormant and the spirit realm is very close to us. The winter solstice marks the shortest day of the year and brings about the end of a season and the promise of renewal in days to come.

The Winter Solstice is unique as it brings the longest night and the shortest day. The dark triumphs but only briefly, for the Solstice is also a turning point. Even as the dark seems to have taken over, the nights actually grow shorter and the days longer. For now, however, we dwell in the dark season. There is much to be discovered if we can slow down, sit back, and give ourselves time to fully experience this annual period of rest and renewal.

Many of the customs associated with the Winter Solstice (and other midwinter festivals such as St. Lucy's Day, Saturnalia, Hanukkah, New Year's and Twelfth Night) derive from stories of a mighty battle between the dark and the light, which is won, naturally, by the light. Other traditions record this as the time a savior (the Sun-Child) is born to a virgin mother.

The Battle Between Old and New, Dark and Light

The Romans celebrated Saturnalia from December 17th to December 24th, during which time all work was put aside in favor of feasting and gambling. The social order was reversed, with masters waiting on their slaves. The Saturnalia is named after Saturn, who is often depicted with a sickle like the figures of Death or Old Father Time. Astrologically speaking, Saturn is gloomy, old, dutiful and heavy. He ate his own children, rather than let them surpass him. For new life to flourish, for the sun to rise again, this crabby old man must be defeated. The festivals of midwinter combat the forces of gloom.

Saturn today is viewed as a force that leaves no stone unturned. It is the very energy that allows us to look at what we have not dealt with in our lives.

After vanquishing the Old King, it's time to celebrate the new. Thus, the day following the Saturnalia was set aside to honor children. This festival was called the Juvenalia, according to Z Budapest in The Grandmother of Time. The holiday honored children with entertainment, lavish meals, and presents of good luck talismans. Naturally this is the time of the year at which the birth of Christ is celebrated, since he is also the New King, the Light of the World who brings light. Another familiar figure from this time of year is the New Year's Baby, who takes over from Old Father Time.

The Birth of the Sun

Christ's birthday was not celebrated on December 25th until the 4th century. Before then, December 25th was best known as the birthday of the Persian hero and sun-god, Mithra. According to myth, he sprang up full-grown from a rock, armed with a knife and carrying a torch. Shepherds watched his miraculous appearance and hurried to greet him with the first fruits of their flocks and their harvests. The cult of Mithra spread all over the Roman Empire. In 274 CE the Roman emperor Valerian declared December 25th the Birthday of Sol Invictus, the Unconquerable Sun.

Christ was also not the first miraculous child said to have been born to a virgin mother. As Marina Warner points out, "The virgin birth of heroes and sages was a widespread formula in the Hellenistic world: Pythagorus, Plato, Alexander were all believed to be born of woman by the power of a holy spirit."

The union of a virgin and a supernatural force, such as the couplings between Zeus and various nymphs, was shorthand indicating the presence of a miraculous child, a child with the powers of both worlds. Dionysus is such a child, born of a union between Zeus and Semele.

H. W. Parke in Festivals of the Athenians describes a women-only midwinter festival, the Lenaia, which honored Dionysos. On this night, Greek women "held their ecstatic dances in winter—fully clothed in Greek dress, with castanets or the thyrsus, dancing together with no male companions, human or satyr." Robert Graves calls it the Lenaea, the Festival of Wild Women (a nice companion for the Festival of Merry Women on December 14).

A bull, representing Dionysus, was cut into nine pieces, with one piece being burned and the rest consumed raw by the worshippers. Dionysus was born in winter, crowned with serpents, became a lion in the spring and was sacrificed as a bull (or a stag or goat) in the summer because these were calendar emblems of the old tripartite year. Marija Gimbutas in Goddesses and Gods of Old Europe calls Dionysus a Year God. Mithra was also associated with the bull (his initiates were baptized with the blood of a sacrificed bull) and shown with the emblems of the zodiac surrounding him, suggesting that he is also a Year God.

The Lenaia occurred on the twelfth day of the Greek lunar month, Gamelion, which falls in early winter. The twelfth day of a lunar month (which begins with the new moon) always falls on a full moon night. If we move this lunar festival to the solar calendar and count from the winter solstice, the festival would occur on January 5th or 6th.

Until the fourth century, Christ's birthday was celebrated on January 6th, on the same date when the Virgin Kore gave birth to the year god; this was celebrated in Alexandria with a festival called the Koreion. St. Epiphanius complains about the hideous mockery of this rite, but it preceded the story of Christ's birth. In the original ceremony, the image of the goddess, decorated with gold stars, was carried seven times around her temple as the priests cried, "The Virgin has brought forth the new Aeon!"

Aeon, or Eon, is now defined as "an indefinitely long period of time" but its Indo-European root aiw means "vital force, life, long life, eternity," and the Greek form Aion meant specifically "vital force." [Farias]

This description recalls the Egyptian ceremony re-enacting the birth of Horus, the sun-god to Isis. All lights in the city were doused while Isis circled the sarcophagus seven times, then brought forth Horus, who was called "the Light of the World." Statues of Isis holding the newly born sun god on her lap, presenting him to the world, are similar in pose to later statues representing Mary and Jesus.

Earth Ways: Ceremony to Re-create your Life

Make a list of what you want. Keep it basic. If you need details, make them simple.

Take your list outside to a favorite tree and stand facing the tree.
Feel the energy of the Earth coming up into your feet, legs and body.

Feel the Universe's energy coming down through the top of your head.

Announce to the tree, the Earth and the Universe what your list holds.

Offer this list to the Universe by wrapping it in a cloth and putting it in the Earth, under a rock or inside the tree.

Ask that your desire to create your life anew be in accordance with the will of the Goddess and the Universe and that what you are asking for is in alignment with your karmic past and your soul's purpose.

Thank the Earth, the Universe and the tree for hearing your list and your prayer and feel all of

it release from your body so you are not holding onto it anymore.

Watch what manifests and remember it is the Universe that directs, choreographs and produces our wants, needs and desires. It is when we think we know what is best for us without looking at our soul's purpose that we get disappointed and feel let down. Stay connected to the path of your soul.

Often during the winter, we find our bodies slowing to the natural rhythm of the Earth: shorter days and less daylight bring more sleep. Use this simple prayer before bed.

Earth Ways: Prayer for Sleep

I am grateful for the rest my body receives when held and comforted by you, Mother Earth. I ask that you keep me safe and protected while I sleep and allow the gentle drumming of your heartbeat to lull me to slumber if I am anxious or stressed. Thank you, Goddess, for your healing and rejuvenation of my body and soul as I sleep to the rhythm of your heart.

Earth Ways: Prayer for the Winter Solstice

Thank you, Mother Earth, for this sacred time where we experience the longest night and the shortest day. As the dark triumphs--but only briefly--we are in gratitude for the Solstice as it marks the turning point to the light. From now until the Summer Solstice as the nights grow shorter and the days grow longer, as the dark wanes and the Sun waxes in power, I will pray to you, Goddess, for your continued good health, clean water, clean air, abundance of crops and the

understanding for humanity to care for you with love. From the dark womb of the night, the light is born and I am forever grateful to you for all that you provide. I send my love into this sacred Earth and to all of humanity for the light that is born on this Winter Solstice to also illuminate our minds and our hearts.

The Dark of Winter

From the beginning of time the duality has defined the Universe. Investing in this constant display of good and bad, right and wrong, dark and light has captured the human experience.   Inside the hearts of humanity there exists a timeless dance with the dark side that yearns to be tempered with the light.   The hearts and minds of all people are one at the core. F ear and the vast differences of belief systems, both personal and cultural, mark the psychology of individuals and keep us apart. The outer workings of the body are as complex as the inner; the only difference is that the inner remains unseen. We have never misplaced the knowledge that stays in our souls, but the experience of being human keeps us so distracted that we tend to forget.

On this shortest day of the year, where we get so close to darkness and are saved by the light of the coming season, let us remember who we are and why we are here on the Earth. Let us question our thinking and examine what we think we know and what our soul remembers. The unseen forces in the Universe are trying to survive, just the same as humans, and they feel as much right to their existence as people do. Honoring the unknown becomes more difficult as humanity reaches a high level of technology around the world. Now that we are at the top of the food chain, we forget what survival once was here on Earth. Our fight or flight mode is still active in us and often saves us from other dark forces. But arrogance and jealousy are the stumbling stones in the pathway of humanity and their egos.

It is in the darkness that we must shine our own light and illuminate our minds, comfort our fears and remember our soul's memory. In doing so we temper the ego and our desire to polarize with the energy that technology has brought to our world.

The journey of your spirit while living in a physical body is the process of awakening and realizing your potential. Each one of us feels our feelings at a deep level--that is the human experience. Feeling the emotional body keeps us connected to the Earth. She feels everything and has a wealth of knowledge that she offers freely if we just allow ourselves to tune in. She gives us signs throughout each season and provides a vast array of experiences to draw upon.

Earth Ways: Ceremony for Winter Solstice

Stand in front of a tree and place your hands on its sleeping trunk. Ask that your prayers be taken deep into the Earth as the tree slumbers until spring. Ask for the Goddess to hear your voice, for you are aware of the sleep that occupies all living things.

Tell her you are grateful for this passage. Tell her you will remain constant and aware of the moon until spring brings all things back to life. Tell her you will walk quietly on the Earth, honoring her in such a way that does not disturb her natural rhythms. Finally, tell her that you will begin anew

with this ceremony and in gratitude; you will begin your life with the promise of spring.

Feel your love going through the mighty tree to the Earth, filling her up with the energy she will need for the coming birth of the Equinox. As an offering of your love and dedication to the Earth leave a small handful of food (nuts and berries, grains and oats) on the ground by the base of the trunk to feed the spirit of the tree and the Earth.

Earth Ways: Ceremony for the Angels

Sitting in meditation, ask for the highest angels to come to you in accordance with the will of the Universe and the Goddess. Ask for these angels to help you clear away any negative energy or any negative thought forms and transmute them into light and love. Ask these angels to give you a message or healing that will help you in your life. Thank the angels for assisting you and ask if they might help those in need around the world. In gratitude thank the Universe for the generosity of the angelic realm.

Winter and the Stars

In icy cold conditions we turn toward the sky and follow the stars and placement of the Big Dipper. In other parts of the world, these seven stars were known not as a Dipper, but as a wagon. In Ireland, for instance, it was recognized as "King David's Chariot," from one of that island's early kings; in France, it was the "Great Chariot." Another popular name was Charles's Wain (a wain being a large open farm wagon). And in the British Isles, these seven stars are known widely as "The Plough."

The Big Dipper or Plough is probably the most important and easily recognizable group of stars in the sky. For anyone in the latitude of New York State (41 degrees North) or points northward, it never goes below the horizon.

For those who live in the Southern Hemisphere, the constellation known as Crux, or the Southern Cross, is the guide to the night sky. Those south of the equator need only cast a glance toward the south to see the distinctive shape of the Cross hanging well up in the sky.

Earth Ways: Prayer for the Night

As we lay our heads down to rest it is with gratitude that we thank you, Mother Earth, for this beautiful day and all that you have given us with your generous abundance, love and warmth. As the night sky comes to touch upon your earth, we pray for your protection and remain forever in gratitude to you for all that you give us. When we close our eyes to rest we entrust you, Goddess, to keep us safe and in your care until the light of dawn brings us a new day. Our bodies are tired and we welcome the rest under your night sky.

Earth Ways: Ceremony for the Earth

Stand outside and quietly thank the Earth for all she provided during the past year. Feel your energy grounding into her right through the soles of your feet. Say your prayers into your hand, as if you are holding the words cupped in your palm. Place your hand on the Earth, and release your prayers with a hand motion that sweeps across the Earth. This is where heaven and Earth meet and your prayers are sprinkled in between.

I sat under the sky with a perfect view of the Milky Way. I was enveloped in the night air as I heard footsteps approaching. I was in a place no one was ever allowed, and where I sat was as old as the artifacts underneath me. It was a magical time as the stars danced above. But the spirits of the night were ever-present; without warning they approached me as they ushered in their final warning. I had to leave now or stay forever.

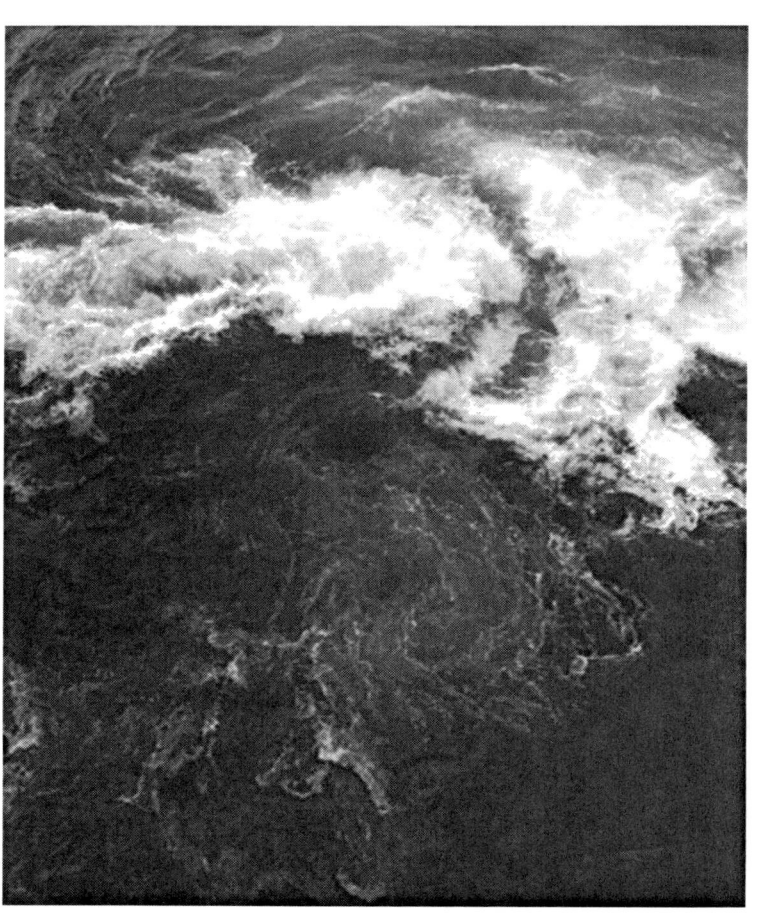

Healing Medicine for the Soul

Healing medicine for the soul is the healing we experience when we fully understand our true, natural form. The soul or spirit body is our natural state of being and we are given the opportunity to experience love at the deepest level of our beings here on Earth. The homework is to feel our feelings and process that information in the physical, mental, emotional and spiritual realms.

We have many ways of learning that can help us to process our experience here on Earth. Hearing what is being said, seeing what you are being shown, feeling the energy and mentally processing the information are the four main learning modalities we can identify with. We experience life through a primary and secondary learning mode. Finding your primary and secondary learning modes will tell you how you best communicate and receive information.

In healing ourselves at a soul level, we must first understand how we take the world in. The processing can become a bit easier with that template in mind. We are bombarded visually throughout school and most of the world operates in a visual mode. If the primary learning modality is tonal but a child receives the world first through her ears and second through the kinesthetic (feeling) mode, she might miss the whole visual presentation that the world is serving up. Often this can result in poor school work and being gifted in the area of music and art.

Effective communication with yourself and your community is based on how each person receives information. Starting with your family and your children, discern if you tend to be visual. Do you say things like, "Don't you see what I mean?" If your child is tonal and hears your words but does not see it, you are missing each other and the process.

The healing medicine for this experience is to observe what you are saying and doing, and from those four learning modalities identify your primary and secondary communication modes by what you feel. Then observe your child and ask how he or she feels, thinks, sees or hears things. If you differ, then honor that and work within their language. A tonal child would need statements of "I hear you." The mental processer might lean heavily on "What do you think? I think this, because of that." Once we have this understood, then the healing can begin.

Practice with your family speaking to each other in the language you all might have in common. You may have kinesthetic as a secondary learning modality. Your spouse and your child may also have this primary or secondary modality; you all have a communication bridge for understanding, which is how you feel about things. Use those words that will help another hear, see, feel or think your point! If you are not being understood, then reassess your language to adjust to the other person's primary or secondary learning modality. This will open up the channels for everyone to feel their feelings, because it is now an environment where everyone feels heard.

There is another layer to healing on a soul level. The duality is an ongoing experience of good and bad, right and wrong, hot and cold, love and hate, and that is how our reality is defined. The key to understanding the duality is to observe it. If we jump in and participate, we are investing on a karmic level and creating more karma in our Earth experience.

Karma is the unresolved and unfinished feelings we have from our past lives. We all have experiences in past lives where we did not get resolved in an interaction with a loved one or a friend. Perhaps we died unexpectedly and could not comprehend that we would die in such a manner. Whatever is not completed on an emotional level within ourselves brings us to experience these unfinished emotional pieces in this lifetime. We attract karmic experiences through manifesting the people we have been historically connected to. This is what people often refer to as a soul mate. There are many soul mates to our karmic configuration and we are bound to these people and events until the issue is cleared.

The key to clearing any karma is forgiveness. We have the power within each of us to forgive in this lifetime everyone who has ever caused us pain or wrongdoing. Karma is repeated so we can heal. It is not a punishment from God and the Universe. The healing process for the soul is to feel our feelings. The bigger picture for your lifetimes of experience is to forgive all throughout your past lives. Once we start forgiving others, we are able to ingest the real medicine for the soul: forgiving ourselves. We tend to criticize ourselves from a place of deep patterning and learned behavior. Seeing through the layers of the human condition, we start to recognize the patterns of what we experienced in this lifetime and our past lives, enriching us with knowledge to feel our feelings and clear through forgiveness.

This process is necessary so we can heal and be available at every moment of every day to love at the deepest level of our beings. Imagine how much you love your mother or father or your children. Feel that feeling in your body and now feel that amount of love for everyone in the world. That is truly the opportunity we are given through each incarnation here on Earth. Our families are simply the learning ground for our much bigger Earth family.

Earth Ways: Purpose

There are many things we desire in life:
Things we want to have,
Things we aspire to do.
Our real purpose is to take care of this planet.
To love her as we love our own mothers.

We are the caretakers of this sacred Earth.
May we reconnect with our purpose and help her
and the next seven generations.

About the Author:

For over thirty years, mystic healer, Sonja Grace has been offering her clients, both in the United States and abroad, immediate stability, clarity and guidance through her readings, counseling and processing work. Sonja has a wide variety of talent to choose from in which she accesses her ability to channel and communicate with the divine. Sonja Grace sees and receives messages from loved ones who have crossed over and offers a venue for healing in this world and the spirit world, thru her spiritual guidance. Sonja works with all of clients over the phone and provides healing in the physical, mental, emotional and spiritual bodies. "Time and space are not what we perceive them to be" Sonja lives with her husband and two cats in Portland, Oregon.

References

http://schooloftheseasons.com/celsolstice.html

http://www.schooloftheseasons.com/spring.html

http://www.ngwa.org/programs/educator/lessonplans/earthwater.aspx

http://schooloftheseasons.com/celsolstice.html

http://www.schooloftheseasons.com/midsummer.htm

CPSIA information can be obtained at www.ICGtesting.com
Printed in the USA
LVOW041416210113

316581LV00001B/41/P